THE AUSTRALIAN
Women's Weekly
bake & cook
with kids

THE AUSTRALIAN
Women's Weekly

contents

playing it safe... 4

We all know how difficult it can be to kids to eat what you want them to. If you get the kids involved in the process of creating food, sharing and eating their results can make everything that much easier. Everybody loves rolling out pastry and baking, so we have some easy options to choose from; then you can move on to the business of preparing vegetables and cooking real main course dishes...

playing it safe...

Here are some basic tips for playing it safe in the kitchen with kids. These simple guidelines will ensure the experience stays fun for everyone.

before you begin

Make sure there is an adult supervising in the kitchen at all times. Also make sure you read the recipe through together a few times before you start preparing. Have all the ingredients and utensils you need ready to go.

clean hands

Hands should always be washed with soap and warm water (don't forget your fingernails) and dried on a clean towel or paper towel. This is extremely important when you are handling uncooked food. Before making sandwiches, cutting a fruit salad or tossing salad vegetables, always wash your hands thoroughly. If someone has a cut on their hand, they should wear disposable gloves. Hands should always be washed after touching any uncooked meat, seafood or poultry.

personal hygiene

No-one should touch their hair or mouth, or leave the kitchen to do something else, without washing their hands again before touching any food. Remember to stay out of the kitchen if you're sick.

clothing to wear

Kids (and adults!) should wear short-sleeved or tight-fitting, long-sleeved tops. Loose-fitting ones can drop into the food, or worse, catch fire over a hot stove.

feet first

Everyone should wear closed-toed shoes when cooking (more than one chef has dropped a sharp knife, point-first, onto his or her toes). It's not a bad idea to wear non-slip shoes as well.

defrosting your meat

Always thaw meat, seafood and poultry, covered, in the refrigerator. In a pinch, you can defrost these items in your microwave oven, but take care because some outside edges of the meat can actually cook. Place meat on a tray in the refrigerator as it defrosts to stop it dripping onto other food.

keep hair out of the way

Tie long hair back to keep it from falling into the food or onto food preparation surfaces. It will also prevent singeing from any wayward strands. This is why most chefs wear hats!

taste the food

It's a good idea to taste food as you prepare it, to test for flavour, but don't taste from the stirring spoon or salad fork, then return it to the saucepan or serving bowl. Use different, clean cutlery every time you taste. And, don't add salt to enhance the flavour – your idea of perfect seasoning may be far too much for someone else.

tidy up as you go

Keep work surfaces clean and tidy as you go. Wipe up any spills or grease spots that occur during cooking. Never use the same cloth to wipe your hands and to clean the benchtops. Rinse the cloth constantly in hot soapy water. And, if you wash any equipment you've used, you can use it again to make something else. Even if you don't use it again, at least the food won't cement itself to the bottom of the utensils.

put stuff away

Put the food you've finished with back in the refrigerator or pantry, checking first to make sure that lids are on tight. With uncooked meat, seafood or poultry, ensure it's wrapped tightly in cling film or placed in a sealable bag or an airtight container. The same applies to raw vegetables. Wrap them tightly and return them to the crisper in the fridge.

A is for...

apple turnovers

makes 8
preparation 15 minutes, plus chilling time
cooking 30 minutes

40g butter
3 Granny Smith apples, peeled, cored, finely chopped
2 tablespoons maple syrup
1 tablespoon caster sugar
½ teaspoon ground cinnamon
¼ cup (80g) sultanas
2 sheets frozen puff pastry, thawed
1 egg, lightly beaten
icing sugar, ice-cream, to serve

step 1 Melt butter in a large frying pan over a medium heat. Cook apple, stirring occasionally, for 4-5 minutes until tender. Stir in maple syrup, sugar, and cinnamon. Cook, stirring, for 4-5 minutes until liquid boils and thickens.

step 2 Transfer mixture to a bowl. Stir in sultanas. Set aside for 15 minutes to cool, then chill until mixture is cold. Preheat oven to hot, 200°C. Cut each pastry sheet into 4 even-sized squares.

step 3 Spoon 2 tablespoons apple mixture onto one half of each pastry square. Brush edges with a little egg. Fold pastry over filling to form a triangle, pressing edges to seal. Brush with remaining egg. Bake for 15-20 minutes until golden. Dust with icing sugar and serve with ice-cream.

...apple

...apple

apple custard slice

makes about 16
preparation 25 minutes
cooking 1 hour

1 cup (150g) plain flour, sifted
½ cup (110g) brown sugar
½ cup (40g) desiccated coconut
125g butter, melted
icing sugar, to dust

FILLING
800g can apple slices
¾ cup (180ml) whipping cream
2 eggs
2 tablespoons caster sugar

TOPPING
½ cup (75g) plain flour
½ cup (70g) slivered almonds
⅓ cup (75g) brown sugar
60g butter, melted

tip
If you like, you can use 1 sheet of shortcrust pastry for the base instead. Prick the base with a fork and bake for 10 minutes before covering with the filling.

step 1 Preheat oven to moderate, 180°C. Lightly grease and line an 18 x 28cm slice tin with baking parchment.
step 2 In a bowl, combine flour, brown sugar and coconut. Blend in butter. Press mixture firmly into prepared tin. Bake for 15-20 minutes until lightly browned. Allow to cool.
step 3 FILLING: Spread apple over base. Whisk together cream, eggs and caster sugar. Pour over apple. Bake for 20-25 minutes until firm.
step 4 TOPPING: In a bowl, combine all the ingredients. Sprinkle evenly over slice. Bake for 12-15 minutes until golden. Allow to cool in tin. Dust with icing sugar and cut into squares to serve.

B is for...

banana smoothie

serves 4
preparation 5 minutes

2 cups milk, chilled
3 ripe bananas, peeled, sliced
4 scoops vanilla ice-cream
½ cup (140g) vanilla (or other flavour) yogurt
1 tablespoon honey
nutmeg, to serve

step 1 Arrange all the ingredients on the work surface.
step 2 Place all ingredients in a blender or food processor.
Process until smooth.
step 3 Transfer to a jug and pour into glasses.
Serve topped with a sprinkling of nutmeg.

...banana

...banana

banana & blueberry bread

makes 1 loaf
preparation 15 minutes
cooking 1 hour

2 cups (300g) plain flour
2 teaspoons baking powder
½ teaspoon ground cinnamon
1 cup (220g) brown sugar
3 medium bananas, mashed
125g butter, melted
2 eggs, lightly beaten
1 teaspoon vanilla extract
¾ cup (110g) fresh or frozen blueberries

step 1 Preheat oven to moderate, 180°C. Lightly grease a
10 x 20cm loaf tin. Line the base with baking parchment.
step 2 Sift flour, baking powder and cinnamon together into a
large bowl. Stir in sugar.
step 3 In a large jug, combine banana, butter, egg and vanilla
extract. Fold into flour mixture with blueberries until combined.
Pour mixture into prepared tin.
step 4 Bake for 55-60 minutes or until a skewer inserted into
centre comes out clean and dry. Cut into slices to serve.

C is for...

Everyone loves cookies — they're the perfect gift for the person who has everything as well as being a great after-school treat and a popular addition at a birthday party feast. So, who did steal the cookie from the cookie jar?

...cookies

...cookies

abc cookies

makes 26
preparation 30 minutes, plus chilling time
cooking 20 minutes

125g butter, at room temperature, chopped
½ cup (110g) caster sugar
1 egg yolk
2 cups (300g) plain flour
1 teaspoon bicarbonate of soda
¼ cup (90g) honey

step 1 Preheat oven to moderate, 180°C. Lightly grease and line 4 baking trays with baking parchment. In a large bowl, using an electric mixer, beat together butter and sugar for 2-3 minutes until creamy. Add egg yolk, beating well. Fold in combined sifted flour and bicarbonate of soda.

step 2 Heat honey in a microwave-safe bowl in the microwave on high (100%) power for 20 seconds. Stir into dough. Mix well. Cover in cling film. Chill for 30 minutes. Knead gently on a lightly floured surface. Roll out between 2 sheets of baking parchment until 0.5cm thick.

step 3 Using 8cm alphabet cutters, cut out letters. Place on prepared trays. Bake for 15-20 minutes until firm to touch. Allow to cool on trays. Spread with icing (see note) and decorate.

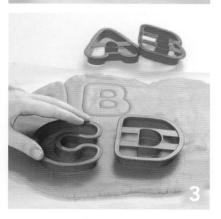

icing
To make icing, beat 1 egg white with a wooden spoon until frothy. Add 1¼ cups (200g) sifted icing sugar, 1 tablespoonful at a time, beating well after each addition. When icing is a piping consistency, mix in a few drops of lemon juice. Add colouring of your choice.

...cookies

smartie cookies

makes about 24
preparation 20 minutes
cooking 10 minutes

125g butter, chopped, at room temperature
½ cup (110g) brown sugar
½ cup (110g) caster sugar
1 egg
1 teaspoon vanilla extract
1¼ cups (185g) plain flour
¼ cup (35g) self-raising flour
½ teaspoon bicarbonate of soda
180g packet Smarties™

tip
These cookies will be soft when cooked, but they will harden on cooling.

step 1 Preheat oven to moderate, 180°C. Lightly grease 2 large baking trays.
step 2 In a large bowl, using an electric mixer, cream butter and sugars together until light and fluffy. Beat in egg and vanilla extract until combined.
step 3 Sift flours and bicarbonate of soda together onto a piece of paper towel. Lightly fold into butter mixture.
step 4 Roll level tablespoonfuls of mixture into balls. Arrange on prepared trays 4cm apart. Using floured fingertips, flatten slightly. Top with Smarties.
step 5 Bake for 10-12 minutes until golden. Allow to cool on trays for 5 minutes. Transfer to a wire rack to cool completely.

...cookies

muesli & coconut cookies

makes about 24
preparation 10 minutes
cooking 20 minutes

125g butter, chopped
¼ cup (55g) brown sugar
¼ cup (90g) honey
1½ cups (190g) untoasted muesli
1 cup (80g) desiccated coconut
½ cup (75g) self-raising flour, sifted
1 teaspoon ground cinnamon

step 1   Preheat oven to moderate, 180°C. Lightly grease and line 2 baking trays. In a small saucepan, heat butter, sugar and honey on low, stirring for 2-3 minutes until combined.
step 2   Meanwhile, mix muesli, coconut, flour and cinnamon together in a large bowl. Add butter mixture, stirring until combined.
step 3   Place tablespoonfuls of mixture onto prepared trays 3cm apart. Flatten slightly. Bake for 15-18 minutes until golden. Cool on trays for 5 minutes before transferring to a wire rack to cool completely. Store in an airtight container.

tip
When measuring honey, spray the inside of the measuring cup lightly with oil. The honey will then pour out easily without the need for a spatula.

D is for...

guacamole with tortilla crisps & vegetable sticks

makes about 2 cups
preparation 10 minutes
cooking 10 minutes

6 flour tortillas
vegetable sticks of choice (carrot, celery, green beans,
    peppers, spring onions, radishes)
GUACAMOLE
2 ripe avocados, halved, stones removed, peeled
1 onion, finely chopped
1 large tomato, chopped
¼ cup (60ml) light sour cream
juice 1 lime or ½ lemon
1 garlic clove, crushed

step 1 Preheat oven to moderate, 180°C. Line a baking tray with baking paper. Arrange tortillas on prepared tray. Spray with oil.
step 2 Bake for 5-10 minutes or until crisp, then allow to cool. Break tortillas into pieces.
step 3 GUACAMOLE: In a bowl, lightly mash avocado with a fork and blend in all remaining ingredients. Season to taste. Serve as a dip for tortilla crisps and vegetable sticks.

tip
For easy mashing it is important that the avocados are very ripe.

...dips

...dips

tuna & beetroot dip with pitta crisps

makes about 2 cups
preparation 5 minutes

450g can whole baby beetroot, drained
125g packet cream cheese, at room temperature, chopped
1 garlic clove, chopped
185g can tuna in springwater, drained, flaked
2 tablespoons chopped chives
pitta bread, toasted, to serve

step 1 Place beetroot, cream cheese and garlic in a food
processor or blender. Process until smooth.
step 2 Stir through tuna and chives. Serve the dip with toasted
pitta bread.

E is for...

...eggs

The staple of many a hearty breakfast, eggs are probably the most versatile, essential ingredient you will use. Before using eggs in a recipe, break one at a time into a small saucer, that way, a stale egg can be discarded, rather than ruin the whole dish.

...eggs

egg bake

makes 4
preparation 10 minutes
cooking 30 minutes

2 teaspoons vegetable oil
2 rashers rindless bacon, finely chopped
½ small red onion, finely chopped
125g cherry tomatoes, halved
8 eggs
⅔ cup (80g) grated cheddar cheese
2 tablespoons finely chopped chives
2 tablespoons finely chopped parsley

step 1 Preheat oven to moderately low, 160°C. Lightly grease
4 x 1½-cup ramekins. Arrange on a baking tray. Heat oil in a
medium frying pan on high. Sauté bacon and onion for
3-4 minutes until onion is tender. Add tomato and cook 1 minute.
Allow to cool.
step 2 In a bowl, combine bacon mixture, 4 eggs, half the cheese,
chives and parsley. Season to taste. Divide evenly between
prepared ramekins.
step 3 Break remaining eggs, one at a time, into a small bowl.
Carefully slide one into each dish. Sprinkle each evenly with
remaining cheese. Bake for 20-25 minutes until the yolk is just set.
Serve immediately.

...eggs

scrambled eggs with bacon & avocado

serves 4
preparation 10 minutes
cooking 10 minutes

4 rindless bacon rashers, trimmed
8 eggs
⅓ cup (80ml) single cream
4 slices wholemeal bread, toasted
1 large avocado, stone removed, mashed
2 tomatoes, sliced
baby spinach leaves, to serve

step 1 Heat a large non-stick frying pan on high. Cook bacon for 3-4 minutes each side, until browned and crisp. Transfer to a plate and cover to keep warm.

step 2 Meanwhile, in a bowl, whisk together eggs and cream. Season to taste. Add egg mixture to pan. Gently stir eggs over low heat for 2-3 minutes until almost set.

step 3 Spread avocado over toast and top with tomato, bacon and egg. Serve topped with spinach and extra pepper, if desired.

tips

If preferred, sauté baby spinach in a small amount of butter for a minute or two, until wilted, before serving. To prevent the avocado from discolouring, add a squeeze of lemon juice and prepare the avocado at the last minute.

F is for...

fish fingers with potato wedges

serves 4
preparation 20 minutes
cooking 35 minutes

4 potatoes, peeled, cut into wedges
1 tablespoon olive oil
600g white skinless boneless fish fillets (such as cod or hake),
    cut crossways into 3cm-wide pieces
¼ cup (35g) seasoned flour
⅓ cup (83ml) milk
1 egg, lightly beaten
1 cup (70g) stale breadcrumbs
mayonnaise, lemon wedges, to serve

step 1 Preheat oven to very hot, 220°C. Line two baking trays with baking parchment. In a large bowl, toss potato in oil. Season to taste. Place in a single layer on one of the prepared trays. Bake for 20 minutes.

step 2 Meanwhile, toss fish in flour and shake off excess. Dip into combined milk and egg. Dip into breadcrumbs, pressing firmly. Place on other tray. Spray with oil.

step 3 Bake fish and potato wedges for a further 10-15 minutes until golden and cooked through, turning fish fingers halfway through cooking. Serve with mayonnaise and lemon wedges.

...fish

G is for...

...gingerbread

Run, run, as fast as you can. You can't catch me, I'm the gingerbread man...
You can use the gingerbread recipe to make all sorts of shaped biscuits – stars, hearts, animals – or use it to construct a gingerbread house for your gingerbread men!

...gingerbread

gingerbread men

makes 8
preparation 20 minutes, plus chilling time
cooking 10 minutes

125g unsalted butter, at room temperature
½ cup (110g) brown sugar
1 egg
2 tablespoons golden syrup
2 cups (300g) plain flour, sifted
2 teaspoons ground ginger
1 teaspoon bicarbonate of soda
½ cup (80g) icing sugar
water
sweets, to decorate

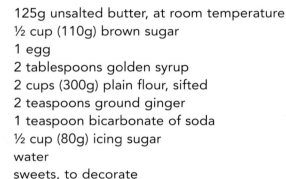

step 1 In a large bowl, using an electric mixer, beat the butter and sugar together until pale and creamy. Add the egg and syrup, then beat until just combined. Sift the flour, ginger and soda together, then fold into the butter mixture until a dough forms.
step 2 Turn the dough onto a lightly floured surface and knead gently until smooth. Wrap in cling film and chill for 2 hours. Preheat oven to moderate, 180°C. Line an oven tray with baking parchment.
step 3 Roll the dough between 2 sheets of baking parchment until about 1cm thick. Using a gingerbread-man cutter, cut 8 shapes from the dough. Place on prepared tray, allowing space for spreading. Bake for 8-10 minutes or until golden. Cool on tray for 5 minutes before transferring to a wire rack to cool completely. Store in an air tight container.

to decorate

Mix the icing sugar with enough water to form a paste. Pipe or spoon eyes and mouths onto gingerbread men, then decorate with sweets of your choice. You could use ready-made decorating icing from the supermarket, if you prefer. You could also try using other cookie cutter shapes for more variety and fun.

H is for...

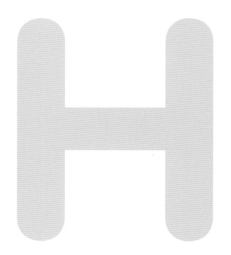

hamburger with the lot

makes 4
preparation 20 minutes, plus chilling time
cooking 10 minutes

500g minced beef
1 small onion, finely chopped
2 tablespoons finely chopped parsley
1 egg, lightly beaten
2 garlic cloves, crushed
1 tablespoon oil
4 slices cheddar cheese
4 bacon rashers
4 bread rolls, halved, toasted
⅓ cup (80ml) tomato sauce
4 round lettuce leaves
2 tomatoes, thinly sliced
potato wedges, to serve (see page 32)

step 1   In a medium bowl, combine beef, onion, parsley, egg and garlic. Season to taste. Shape mixture into 4 evenly-sized flattened burgers. Place on a tray. Cover and chill for 15 minutes until firm.
step 2   Heat oil in a large frying pan on medium. Fry burgers for 3-5 minutes each side until cooked through.
step 3   Top each burger with a slice of cheese. Set aside and cover to keep warm. Fry bacon in the same pan over a high heat for 2-3 minutes each side until crisp. Spread tomato sauce on roll bases. Top each with lettuce, tomato, a burger, bacon and remaining half of roll. Serve hamburgers with wedges.

tip
Try different types of cheeses on your burgers – goat's cheese, blue cheese or gruyère will make your meal more interesting.

...hamburger

I is for...

...ice-cream

I scream, you scream, we all scream for ice-cream...

...ice-cream

ice-cream sandwiches

makes 6
preparation 10 minutes

12 chocolate chip cookies
6 small scoops chocolate ice-cream
crushed peanuts (see note) and
    hundreds and thousands, to coat

step 1 Line a baking tray with baking parchment. Sandwich 2 biscuits together with 1 scoop ice-cream.
step 2 Using a knife, carefully cut away any excess ice-cream.
step 3 Place peanuts and hundreds and thousands in separate bowls. Roll ice-cream sandwiches, upright, in peanuts, then in hundreds and thousands, ensuring ice-cream is evenly coated. Arrange ice-cream sandwiches on tray and freeze until required.

note
Remember to check that no-one has an allergy to nuts.
If you're not sure, use chocolate sprinkles instead of nuts.

...ice cream

vanilla ice-cream

serves 6
preparation 10 minutes,
plus overnight freezing

395g can sweetened condensed milk
300g carton soured cream
3 teaspoons vanilla extract
2 egg whites
ice-cream cones, to serve

step 1 Line a metal cake tin with cling
film. In a large bowl, whisk together
condensed milk, cream and vanilla extract.
step 2 In another bowl, using an electric
mixer, beat egg whites to soft peaks. Fold
into milk mixture. Pour into prepared tin.
step 3 Cover with cling film and freeze
overnight until firm. Serve scoops of ice-
cream in cones.

strawberry sundaes

serves 6
preparation 5 minutes

12 scoops strawberry ice-cream
12 strawberries, hulled, chopped
chocolate sauce

step 1 Place 2 scoops of ice-cream into
each dish.
step 2 Top with strawberries.
step 3 Drizzle with the chocolate sauce
to serve.

tip
These sundaes are extra yummy when
served with ice-cream wafers.

hokey-pokey
ice-cream

serves 6
preparation 5 minutes,
plus overnight freezing

½ litre vanilla ice-cream,
   slightly softened
⅓ cup caramel topping
2 Crunchie bars, chopped

step 1 In a bowl, combine ice-cream,
caramel topping and three-quarters of the
Crunchie bars. Mix well.
step 2 Spoon into a metal cake tin. Cover
and freeze overnight until firm.
step 3 Serve scoops of ice-cream topped
with remaining Crunchie bars

rainbow
ice-cream

serves 6
preparation 5 minutes,
plus overnight freezing

½ litre vanilla ice-cream,
   softened slightly
½ cup coloured sprinkles
ice-cream cones, to serve

step 1 In a large bowl, combine the ice-
cream and sprinkles.
step 2 Spoon into a metal cake tin.
step 3 Cover and freeze overnight until
firm. Serve scoops of rainbow ice-cream in
cones.

...ice-cream

watermelon sorbet

makes 6 cups
preparation 5 minutes, plus overnight freezing
cooking 15 minutes

1 cup caster sugar
1½ cups (375ml) water
2kg seedless watermelon, skin removed, chopped
4 egg whites
6 paper cups
6 lolly sticks

step 1 Combine the sugar and water in a medium saucepan. Stir over a low heat until the sugar dissolves. Simmer, without stirring, for 10 minutes until the mixture thickens. Remove from the heat and allow to cool in pan.

step 2 Purée watermelon in a blender or food processor. Pour through a sieve. Add to the syrup and stir to combine.

step 3 Pour mixture into a metal cake tin, cover with foil and freeze until almost set. Transfer to a chilled bowl. Add egg whites and beat with an electric mixer for 2-3 minutes until all the ice particles have broken up.

step 4 Divide the sorbet evenly between the paper cups. Insert a lolly stick in the centre of each and continue to freeze overnight until firm.

Jelly on a plate, jelly on a plate,
wibble, wobble, wibble, wobble,
jelly on a plate...

J is for...

...jelly

...jelly

jelly oranges

makes 8
preparation 20 minutes, plus chilling time
cooking 12 minutes

4 oranges
½ cup (110g) caster sugar
3 teaspoons gelatine
½ cup (125ml) just-boiled water

step 1 Cut oranges in half. Juice and strain into a jug. Scrape
flesh from skins. Place skins in a bowl and cover with boiling water.
Stand for 1 minute before draining and rinsing under cold water.
Place on a wire rack and drain well.
step 2 In a small saucepan, combine orange juice and sugar.
Stir over a low heat until sugar dissolves. Bring to the boil over a
high heat. Reduce heat to low and simmer for 10 minutes.
step 3 Place orange halves in 8 recesses of a 12-hole muffin tin.
In a small jug, using a fork, whisk gelatine briskly into just-boiled
water until dissolved. Remove from heat. Blend gelatine mixture
into orange mixture in tin. Pour into orange skins. Chill for 3 hours
or overnight until set. Serve whole or cut into wedges.

tip
Make these a day in advance to ensure they are well chilled
and firm.

...jelly

jelly parfaits

makes 10
preparation 30 minutes
plus chilling time

85g packet berry blue jelly
10 plastic wine goblets
250g packet mini jam rolls, cut into 1cm slices
85g packet orange jelly
85g packet strawberry jelly
whipped cream and berries to serve

step 1 Make blue jelly according to packet instructions. Pour blue jelly into base of goblets. Chill for 2 hours until firm.
step 2 Cover with 1 layer sponge, trimming to cover jelly. Make orange jelly according to packet instructions. Chill for 30 minutes until thickened slightly.
step 3 Pour over sponge layer. Chill for 1 hour 30 minutes until firm. Cover with another layer of sponge and strawberry jelly (also slightly set). Cover and chill for 1½ hours until firm. Serve topped with whipped cream and berries.

K is for...

chicken kebabs with potato & pesto

makes 12
preparation 20 minutes
cooking 25 minutes

1kg baby new potatoes, unpeeled
50g butter, chopped
1 tablespoon milk
500g chicken breast, cut into 2cm cubes
1 courgette, halved lengthways, sliced
1 baby aubergine, sliced
½ red pepper, deseeded, cut into 2cm cubes
½ yellow pepper, deseeded, cut into 2cm cubes
6 bamboo skewers, halved (see tip)
1 tablespoons olive oil
ready-made pesto, to serve

step 1 Cook potatoes in a saucepan of boiling, salted water for 15-20 minutes until tender. Drain. Transfer half the potatoes to a medium bowl. Mash with butter and milk until smooth. Roughly mash remaining potatoes. Fold into mash mixture. Season to taste. Keep warm.
step 2 Meanwhile, thread chicken and vegetables alternately onto skewers. Brush with oil and season to taste.
step 3 Spray a char-grill with oil. Preheat on medium. Cook skewers for 3-5 minutes each side until chicken is cooked through. Serve with mash and pesto.

tip
Soak the skewers in water for at least an hour to prevent them from splintering and scorching.

...kebabs

...kebabs

lamb kebabs

makes 8
preparation 20 minutes,
plus marinating time
cooking 12 minutes

500g lamb fillet, cubed
⅓ cup (80ml) vegetable stock
1 tablespoon Dijon mustard
1 garlic clove, crushed
16 cherry tomatoes
1 red onion, cut into wedges
8 bamboo skewers, soaked
couscous, to serve

step 1   In a bowl, combine lamb, stock,
mustard and garlic. Season to taste.
Marinate for 30 minutes.
step 2   Thread lamb, tomatoes and onion
onto skewers. Char-grill or barbecue
skewers for 10-12 minutes, turning, until
cooked to taste. Serve with coucous.

lime fish kebabs

makes 8
preparation 15 minutes
cooking 10 minutes

finely grated rind and juice 1 lime
1 garlic clove, crushed
600g tuna, cubed
1 red pepper, deseeded, cubed
8 bamboo skewers, soaked
cooked rice, lime wedges, to serve

step 1   In a bowl, combine lime rind, lime
juice and garlic. Add tuna. Cover. Chill for
10 minutes.
step 2   Thread tuna and pepper onto
skewers. Season to taste. Chargrill skewers
for 8-10 minutes, turning, until cooked
through. Serve with rice and lime wedges.

tip
Try prawns instead of tuna in this recipe.

note
Soak the skewers in water for at least an hour to prevent them from splintering and scorching.

chicken kebabs

makes 16
preparation 10 minutes, plus chilling time
cooking 15 minutes

500g chicken breast fillets, cut into
    16 strips
16 bamboo skewers, soaked
¼ cup (60ml) mirin
2 tablespoons brown sugar
2 tablespoons soy sauce
1 spring onion, sliced thinly

step 1 Thread chicken onto skewers.
Place in a baking dish with mirin, sugar
and soy sauce. Chill overnight.
step 2 Chargrill skewers, reserving
marinade, for 8-10 minutes, turning, until
cooked through.
step 3 Simmer reserved marinade for
3-5 minutes until thickened. Drizzle over
skewers. Top with sliced onion.

cheese & ham kebabs

makes 8
preparation 20 minutes
cooking 10 minutes

1 loaf ciabatta bread, cubed
¼ cup (60ml) olive oil
8 bamboo skewers, soaked
16 slices shaved ham, folded
250g haloumi cheese, cubed
8 cherry tomatoes

step 1 Toss bread in oil. Thread bread
and remaining ingredients onto skewers.
step 2 Char-grill skewers for 8-10 minutes,
turning, until golden.

tip
For a vegetarian option, replace the ham
with pieces of green pepper or onion.

...kebabs

fruit kebabs with passionfruit dip

makes 12
preparation 20 minutes

1 punnet strawberries
½ canteloupe melon, peeled, deseeded, cut into chunks
¼ seedless watermelon, cut into chunks
¼ pineapple, cut into chunks
2 bananas, thickly sliced
2 kiwifruit, peeled, quartered
12 bamboo skewers or straws
PASSIONFRUIT DIPPING SAUCE
1 cup (280g) vanilla yogurt
¼ cup (60ml) passionfruit pulp

step 1 Thread fruit chunks alternately onto skewers. Set aside.
step 2 PASSIONFRUIT DIPPING SAUCE: In a jug, combine yogurt and passionfruit. Drizzle over fruit kebabs to serve.

tip
For a delicious variation, replace the passionfruit in the dipping sauce with 1 tablespoon of honey or chocolate sauce.

L is for...

lemon delicious

serves 4
preparation 20 minutes
cooking 35 minutes

50g butter
¾ cup (165g) caster sugar
finely grated zest and juice 2 lemons
4 eggs, separated
¼ cup (35g) self-raising flour
1¼ cups (310ml) milk
icing sugar, for dusting
cream and lemon peel strips, to serve

step 1 Preheat oven to moderately low, 160°C. Lightly grease 4 x 1-cup ramekins. In a large bowl, using an electric mixer, cream the butter, half the sugar and all the zest together until light and fluffy. Beat in egg-yolks and flour. Gradually beat in lemon juice and milk, until well combined.

step 2 In a clean bowl, using an electric mixer, beat egg-whites until soft peaks form. Gradually add remaining sugar until the mixture is thick and glossy. Gently fold through lemon mixture. Pour evenly between prepared ramekins.

step 3 Place ramekins in a large baking pan. Fill baking dish with boiling water until it comes halfway up the sides of the ramekins. Bake for 30-35 minutes until firm and golden. Dust with icing sugar. Serve with cream. Top with lemon strips, if desired.

tip
It will take about 1 hour to cook if using 1 large dish. This dish is quite saucy in the base.

...lemon

citrus mousse

serves 6
preparation 15 minutes
cooking 10 minutes
chilling 2 hours+

1 cup (220g) caster sugar
2 tablespoons each: lemon juice, lime juice, orange juice
2 teaspoons each: lemon rind, orange rind, lime rind
3 teaspoons gelatine
¼ cup (60ml) boiled water
2 egg whites
300ml whipping cream, lightly whipped
whipped cream, rind and wafer biscuits, to serve

step 1 In a medium saucepan, combine sugar and juices. Stir over a low heat, until sugar dissolves. Bring to boil. Simmer, without stirring, for 5 minutes. Remove from heat. Stir in citrus rinds. Cool to room temperature. Transfer to a large bowl.

step 2 In a small bowl, whisk gelatine briskly into water until dissolved. Cool to room temperature. Whisk into juice mixture.

step 3 Beat egg whites in a clean bowl until soft peaks form. Fold into juice mixture with cream. Spoon into 6 x ½-cup ramekins. Chill for 2 hours or overnight until firm. Decorate tops with whipped cream and rind. Serve with biscuits.

tip
It is important to have the mixtures at similar temperatures before combining, to prevent strings and lumps.

M is for...

Do you know the muffin man, the muffin man, the muffin man ...

Muffins are so easy to make; if you use silicone or non-stick bakeware, they are very easy to lift from the tins – and they are sooooooo good to eat warm, shared with friends or your kitchen helpers. You can store the rest of the cooled muffins in an airtight container and eat them over the next couple of days. Once you have made them a couple of times, experiment with your own favourite flavours!

...muffins

choc-caramel surprise muffins

makes 12
preparation 15 minutes
cooking 25 minutes

2 cups (300g) self-raising flour
½ cup (110g) caster sugar
½ cup (50g) finely chopped pecans
100g dark chocolate, grated
⅔ cup (165ml) milk
125g butter, melted
1 egg, lightly beaten
6 soft caramel sweets, halved

step 1 Preheat oven to moderate, 180°C. Lightly grease a 12-hole muffin tin. Sift flour into a large bowl. Stir in sugar, pecans and chocolate.
step 2 In a jug, whisk together milk, butter and egg. Make a well in the centre of flour mixture. Add milk mixture all at once. Mix lightly until just combined – don't over-mix.
step 3 Spoon enough mixture into each recess of prepared tin to half fill. Top each with half a caramel. Cover evenly with remaining muffin mixture. Bake for 20-25 minutes or until a skewer inserted into the centre comes out clean and dry. Transfer to a wire rack to cool.

tip
To experience the surprise inside, these muffins are best served warm. Other sweets of choice, such as Rolos or squares of Caramel chocolate, can be used.

...muffins

...muffins

cheesy sweet potato muffins

makes 12
preparation 15 minutes
cooking 30 minutes

2 cups (300g) self-raising flour, sifted
1 cup (180G) grated sweet potato, firmly
  packed
2 tablespoons snipped chives
⅔ cup (165ml) buttermilk
125g butter, melted
1 egg, lightly beaten
125g cheddar cheese, cut into 12 cubes

step 1 Preheat oven to 180°C. Combine
flour, sweet potato and half the chives.
step 2 Add buttermilk, butter and egg.
Mix lightly. Spoon into a greased muffin
tin. Press a cube of cheese into each.
step 3 Sprinkle with remaining chives.
Bake for 25-30 minutes.

honey & oat muffins

makes 12
preparation 10 minutes
cooking 25 minutes

2½ cups (375g) self-raising flour, sifted
1 cup (220g) caster sugar
1 cup (90g) rolled oats
90g butter
½ cup (180g) honey
1¼ cups (310ml) buttermilk
1 egg, lightly beaten

step 1 Preheat oven to 180°C. Combine
flour, sugar and ¾ cup (65g) oats.
step 2 Melt butter and honey together.
Add to flour mixture with buttermilk
and egg.
step 3 Spoon into a greased muffin tin.
Sprinkle with oats. Bake for 20-25 minutes.

marshmallow muffins

makes 12
preparation 15 minutes
cooking 25 minutes

2 cups (300g) self-raising flour, sifted
½ cup (110g) caster sugar
1 cup (150g) frozen mixed berries
⅔ cup (165ml) milk
125g butter, melted
1 egg, lightly beaten
6 pink marshmallows, halved

step 1 Preheat oven to 180°C. Combine flour, sugar and berries.
step 2 Add milk, butter and egg. Spoon half into a greased muffin tin. Top with marshmallow halves. Top with batter. Bake for 20-25 minutes.

cheese, ham & pineapple muffins

makes 12
preparation 15 minutes
cooking 25 minutes

2 cups (300g) self-raising flour, sifted
1 cup (120g) grated cheddar cheese
100g sliced ham, chopped
4 pineapple rings, chopped
3 tablespoons chopped fresh parsley
⅔ cup (165ml) milk
125g butter, melted, cooled
1 egg, lightly beaten

step 1 Preheat oven to 180°C. Combine flour, cheese, ham, pineapple and parsley. Add milk, butter and egg.
step 2 Spoon into a greased muffin tin. Bake for 20-25 minutes.

...omelette

P is for...

...pizza

Do you prefer thick and chewy or thin and crispy? Make your pizza just the way you want it when you make your very own pizza bases from our simple recipe on page 81 – but if you prefer your bases ready-made, then use them to create you very own favourite topping mixture: just the way you like it!

...pizza

pizza faces

makes 4
preparation 10 minutes
cooking 10 minutes

2 small prepared pizza bases
½ cup (125ml) tomato pasta sauce
1 cup (120g) grated mozzarella
8 stuffed olives (for eyes)
4 slices pepperoni (for noses)
4 slices red pepper (for mouths)
8 slices button mushrooms (for ears)
2 slices ham, chopped finely (for hair)

step 1 Preheat oven to hot, 200°C. Line a baking tray with baking parchment. Cut 2 x 12cm rounds from each pizza base.

step 2 Spread each with pasta sauce. Place on prepared tray. Sprinkle with cheese.

step 3 Arrange ingredients on bases to make faces. Bake for 5-10 minutes until golden and the bases are crisp.

...pizza

supreme pizza

makes 2
preparation 15 minutes
cooking 10 minutes

2 cups (300g) self-raising flour
30g butter, chopped
½ cup (125ml) milk
½ cup (125ml) water
TOPPING
⅓ cup (80ml) tomato pasta sauce
1½ cups (180g) grated mozzarella
1 cup (125g) sliced pepperoni
1 red pepper, deseeded, thinly sliced
1 cup (120g) thinly sliced button mushrooms
100g wafer-thin ham, chopped

step 1 Preheat oven to very hot, 220°C. Lightly grease 2 pizza
trays. Sift flour into a bowl. Add butter. Using fingertips, rub in
lightly. Make a well in centre of flour mixture. Pour in combined
milk and water. Using a palette knife, mix quickly to a soft, sticky
dough. Don't over-mix.
step 2 Turn onto a lightly floured surface. Knead lightly. Divide
dough into 2 even-sized pieces. Press or roll out each piece until
large enough to cover pizza trays (see note).
step 3 TOPPING: Spread pizza bases evenly with tomato pasta
sauce. Cover each with cheese and top with an even amount of
pepperoni, pepper, mushroom and ham. Bake for 10-12 minutes
until golden and the bases are crisp. Cut into wedges to serve.

tips
Choose your favourite toppings for this pizza – try sweetcorn, ham,
pineapple, peppers and fresh herbs. This is a scone pizza dough.
We've also used it in the Mexican pizza twists recipe on page 82.

81

...pizza

mexican pizza twists

serves 16
preparation 15 minutes
cooking 15 minutes

1 quantity scone pizza dough
(see Supreme Pizza recipe, page 81)
½ cup (120g) canned refried beans
½ cup (130g) tomato salsa
1 cup (120g) grated cheddar cheese
1 tablespoon chopped parsley
milk, to glaze
sesame seeds, to garnish

step 1 Preheat oven to hot, 200°C. Line 2 baking trays with baking parchment. Divide dough into 16 even-sized pieces. On a lightly floured surface, press or roll out into rounds about 0.5cm thick.
step 2 In a small bowl, combine beans and tomato salsa. Spread evenly over rounds. Top with cheese and parsley.
step 3 Roll up and twist. Place on prepared trays. Brush with milk. Sprinkle with sesame seeds. Bake for 10-15 minutes until the pizza twists are golden.

tip
The pizza twists can be made using pastry as the base – it might be easier for smaller hands to handle.

Q is for...

quesadillas – three ways

serves 4 as a snack
preparation 5 minutes
cooking 5 minutes

2 flour tortillas
BAKED BEANS & CHEESE FILLING
½ cup (150g) baked beans
⅓ cup (40g) grated cheddar cheese
TOMATO, CHEESE & CHUTNEY FILLING
1 tomato, sliced
¼ cup (30g) grated cheddar cheese
2 tablespoons chutney
CHICKEN, CHEESE & SALSA FILLING
¼ cup (40g) shredded cooked chicken
¼ cup (30g) grated cheddar cheese
2 tablespoons tomato salsa

step 1 Heat a frying pan on medium with cooking oil. Place 1 tortilla in pan and top with filling of your choice.
step 2 Cover with the second tortilla and cook for 3-4 minutes, turning once, until golden and crispy.
step 2 Using a lifter, transfer to a chopping board. Serve warm, cut into quarters.

tips
You can make these with sliced sandwich loaf or pitta bread instead of the tortillas. Use a sandwich press, if you like.

...quesadillas

R is for...

rissoles & mash

makes 8
preparation 15 minutes, plus chilling time
cooking 10 minutes

500g lean minced beef
½ cup (35g) fresh breadcrumbs
1 red onion, grated
1 egg
2 tablespoons chopped parsley, plus extra to serve
1 tablespoon barbecue sauce
1 garlic clove, crushed
1 tablespoon olive oil
mashed potato (see tip), green beans, gravy, to serve

step 1 In a bowl, combine mince, breadcrumbs, onion, egg, parsley, barbecue sauce and garlic. Season to taste. Shape mixture into 8 even-sized flattened rissoles.
step 2 Place rissoles on a baking tray and chill for 15 minutes. Heat oil in a large frying pan on medium.
step 3 Cook rissoles for 4-5 minutes each side until golden and cooked through. Drain on paper towel. Serve with mashed potato, green beans (or other vegetables) and gravy of your choice. Sprinkle with extra chopped parsley to serve.

tips
For perfect mash, boil peeled, cubed potatoes for 15-20 minutes until very tender. Drain well. Mash with butter and milk or cream. Season to taste. You could also add grated cheese. Make smaller bite-sized rissoles, if you like.

...rissoles

S is for...

Five fat sausages sizzling in a pan, one went pop and the other went bang...

We all have our favourite sausages – dainty little chipolatas to eat on sticks, or chunky, fat pork sausages. Whichever you like best, cook them very carefully: make sure they are cooked all the way through to the centre, not just browned on the outside. If you're grilling your sausages, make sure they are not too close to the grill, so that they will cook to the middle and if you are frying or barbecuing them, keep the heat medium to low and after a few minutes, turn them over in stages.

...tuna

U is for...

upside-down caramel pear cake

preparation 15 minutes
cooking 35 minutes

125g butter, chopped, at room temperature
1¼ cups (275g) brown sugar
2 firm pears, peeled, thinly sliced lengthways
2 eggs
1 cup (150g) self-raising flour, sifted
1 teaspoon ground cinnamon
⅓ cup (80ml) double cream
thick cream or vanilla ice-cream, to serve

step 1 Preheat oven to moderate, 180°C. Lightly grease a 22cm fluted ring cake tin. In a small saucepan, combine 60g butter and ¾ cup sugar. Stir over low heat for 2-3 minutes until butter melts and mixture is smooth. Pour into cake tin, tilting to cover base.
step 2 Arrange pears in caramel, slightly overlapping. Set aside. In a bowl, using an electric mixer, beat remaining butter and sugar until pale and creamy. Add eggs, one at a time, beating well after each addition. Fold in combined flour and cinnamon. Stir in cream.
step 3 Spoon mixture over pear and smooth top. Bake in preheated oven for 25-30 minutes or until a skewer inserted into the centre comes out clean and dry. Allow to cool in tin for 5 minutes. Turn onto a serving plate. Serve warm or at room temperature, cut into wedges, with cream or ice-cream.

tip
Try other fruit in this recipe – pineapple, apple or orange slices all make delicious alternatives.

V is for...

vegetable & barley soup

serves 4
preparation 10 minutes
cooking 50 minutes

2 carrots, chopped
2 celery stalks, trimmed, chopped
4 cups (1 litre) chicken or vegetable stock
½ cup (100g) pearl barley
2 tablespoons chopped parsley

step 1 Heat a large saucepan on high. Spray with oil and sauté carrots and celery for 4-5 minutes until tender.
step 2 Add stock and barley. Bring to boil. Reduce heat and simmer, covered, for 40-45 minutes until barley is tender. Season to taste.
step 3 Stir parsley through and serve.

tips
If liked, use ½ cup rice or soup pasta instead of barley. Cook rice or pasta for 10-12 minutes until tender. You could also add some chopped potato to soup for the last 20 minutes of cooking.

...vegetables

W is for...

waffles with caramel banana

serves 4
preparation 5 minutes
cooking 20 minutes

1 cup (220g) caster sugar
½ cup (125ml) water
½ cup (120ml) whipping cream
8 frozen waffles, toasted
2 large bananas, diagonally sliced
thick cream, to serve (optional)

step 1 In a saucepan, combine sugar and water. Stir over a medium heat until sugar dissolves. Bring to the boil.
step 2 Reduce heat to low and simmer, without stirring, for around 10-15 minutes until mixture is golden.
step 3 Remove from heat. Whisk in cream. Return pan to low heat and stir until smooth. Top waffles with banana. Pour over caramel to serve. Accompany with cream, if you like.

tip
This caramel sauce is also delicious served over vanilla ice cream, or with fresh fruit and plain yogurt.

...waffles

X is for...

white christmas coconut bites

makes about 36
preparation 10 minutes, plus freezing time
cooking 5 minutes

250g creamed coconut
2 cups (70g) Rice Krispies
1 cup (80g) desiccated coconut
1 cup (160g) icing sugar, sifted
1 cup (100g) milk powder
¾ cup (120g) sultanas
½ cup (60g) chopped red and green jelly sweets
   (jelly babies will do)

step 1 Lightly grease a 20 x 30cm slice tin. Line base and sides
with baking parchment. Place creamed coconut in a small
saucepan. Heat on low, stirring, for 4-5 minutes until melted.
Pour into a jug and allow to cool slightly.
step 2 Meanwhile, combine all the remaining ingredients in a
large bowl. Pour in melted coconut and mix well.
step 3 Press mixture firmly into tin. Freeze 15 minutes or until
set, then chill until ready to serve. Serve cut into small squares.

tip
Creamed coconut is a product made entirely from fresh coconut
and is sold in blocks in supermarkets.

...xmas treats

...xmas treats

shortbread christmas stars

makes about 30
preparation 10 minutes
cooking 20 minutes

2 cups (300g) plain flour
⅓ cup (55g) icing sugar
2 tablespoons rice flour
250g butter, cubed, at room temperature
white chocolate buttons, to decorate
icing sugar, to dust

step 1 Preheat oven to moderately low, 160°C. Line 2 baking trays with baking parchment. Sift flour, icing sugar and rice flour together into a bowl. Using fingertips, rub in butter until the mixture resembles fine breadcrumbs. Press together to form a firm dough.
step 2 Turn onto a floured surface and knead gently. Roll out between 2 sheets baking parchment until 5mm thick.
step 3 Using a 5cm cutter, cut into stars. Arrange on prepared trays. Bake for 15-20 minutes until lightly golden. Remove from oven. Decorate some of the stars with white chocolate buttons. Cool for 5 minutes on trays. Transfer to a rack to cool completely. Dust with icing sugar to serve.

variation
To make dark-chocolate stars, add 60g melted dark chocolate in step 1. Wrap in cling film and chill for 10 minutes. After baking, top with dark chocolate buttons and decorate with silver cachous.

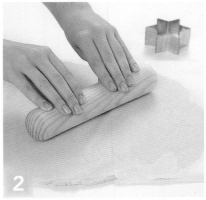

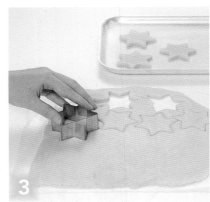

...xmas treats

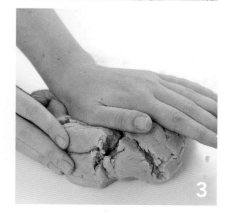

christmas tree biscuits

makes about 20
preparation 30 minutes
cooking 15 minutes

125g butter, chopped, at room temperature
½ cup (110g) caster sugar
1 egg yolk
2 cups (300g) plain flour
3 teaspoons ground ginger
1 teaspoon bicarbonate of soda
¼ cup (90g) golden syrup

step 1 Preheat oven to moderate, 180°C. Lightly grease and line 2 baking trays with baking parchment. In a large bowl, using an electric mixer, beat butter and sugar together for 2-3 minutes until creamy. Add egg yolk, beating well.
step 2 Sift flour, ginger and bicarbonate of soda together. Warm syrup in the microwave on high (100%) power for 20 seconds. Fold flour mixture into butter mixture with syrup to form a dough.
step 3 Knead dough gently on a lightly floured surface. Roll out between 2 sheets of baking parchment until 0.5cm thick. Using cutters, cut out shapes. Place on prepared trays. Bake for 10-15 minutes. Cool on trays. Decorate with icing and cachous.

to decorate
To make icing, beat egg white with a wooden spoon until frothy. Add 1¼ cups (200g) sifted icing sugar, 1 tablespoonful at a time, beating well after each addition. When icing is a piping consistency. Add a few drops of lemon juice and colouring. Pipe and decorate. To turn into tree decorations, make a hole in shapes before baking and thread with ribbon.

...yogurt

Z is for...

butternut squash dip with zoo animal croutons

makes 1 cup
preparation 15 minutes
cooking 20 minutes

500g butternut squash, peeled, cut into
   small cubes, roasted
2 shallots, peeled, quartered
2 tablespoons olive oil, plus extra to brush
6 slices white bread
50g cream cheese, at room temperature

step 1 Preheat oven to a hot, 200°C. Place squash and shallots on a baking tray. Drizzle with oil. Season to taste and toss well. Bake for 15-20 minutes until squash is tender. Allow to cool.
step 2 Meanwhile, using animal shape cookie cutters, cut the bread into shapes. Arrange in a single layer on a baking tray and brush with olive oil. Bake for 4-5 minutes each side until crisp.
step 3 Spoon squash mixture and cream cheese into a food processor or blender. Process until smooth. Season to taste. Serve dip with zoo animal crouton shapes.

tips
If the dip is too thick, add a little water while blending. Use spray oil when making croutons if you like.

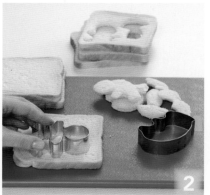

...zoo animals

conversion charts

MEASURES

The cup and spoon measurements used in this book are metric: one measuring cup holds approximately 250ml; one metric tablespoon holds 20ml; one metric teaspoon holds 5ml.

All cup and spoon measurements are level. The most accurate way of measuring dry ingredients is to weigh them. When measuring liquids, use a clear glass or plastic jug with metric markings.

We used large eggs with an average weight of 60g.

WARNING This book may contain recipes for dishes made with raw or lightly cooked eggs. These should be avoided by vulnerable people such as pregnant and nursing mothers, invalids, the elderly, babies and young children.

DRY MEASURES

metric	imperial
15g	½oz
30g	1oz
60g	2oz
90g	3oz
125g	4oz (¼lb)
155g	5oz
185g	6oz
220g	7oz
250g	8oz (½lb)
280g	9oz
315g	10oz
345g	11oz
375g	12oz (¾lb)
410g	13oz
440g	14oz
470g	15oz
500g	16oz (1lb)
750g	24oz (1½lb)
1kg	32oz (2lb)

LIQUID MEASURES

metric	imperial
30ml	1 fl oz
60ml	2 fl oz
100ml	3 fl oz
125ml	4 fl oz
150ml	5 fl oz (¼ pint/1 gill)
190ml	6 fl oz
250ml	8 fl oz
300ml	10 fl oz (½pt)
500ml	16 fl oz
600ml	20 fl oz (1 pint)
1000ml (1 litre)	1¾pints

LENGTH MEASURES

metric	imperial
3mm	⅛in
6mm	¼in
1cm	½in
2cm	¾in
2.5cm	1in
5cm	2in
6cm	2½in
8cm	3in
10cm	4in
13cm	5in
15cm	6in
18cm	7in
20cm	8in
23cm	9in
25cm	10in
28cm	11in
30cm	12in (1ft)

OVEN TEMPERATURES

These oven temperatures are only a guide for conventional ovens. For fan-assisted ovens, check the manufacturer's manual.

	°C (Celcius)	°F (Fahrenheit)	gas mark
Very low	120	250	½
Low	150	275-300	1-2
Moderately low	170	325	3
Moderate	180	350-375	4-5
Moderately hot	200	400	6
Hot	220	425-450	7-8
Very hot	240	475	9

index

Reprinted in 2011.
First Published in 2010 by ACP Magazines Ltd,
a division of PBL Media Pty Limited
54 Park St, Sydney
GPO Box 4088, Sydney, NSW 2001.
phone (02) 9282 8618; fax (02) 9267 9438
acpbooks@acpmagazines.com.au; www. acpbooks.com.au

ACP BOOKS
General Manager Christine Whiston
Director of sales Brian Cearnes
Marketing manager Bridget Cody

Editor Alana House
Art Director Tessa Thomas
Food Director Jennene Plummer
Food Editor Sharon Reeve
Chief Sub-editor Amanda Shaw
Digital Prepress Specialist John Ruperto

Photography: Ian Hoffstetter, Rob Lowe, Andre Martin, Cath Muscat,
Brett Stevens, John Paul Urizar
Styling: Kate Brown, Jane Collins, Kate Nixon, Michelle Noerianto,
Jennene Plummer, Sharon Reeve
Food preparation: Dixie Elliott, Nicole Jennings, Tracy Rutherford,
Mandy Sinclair

The publishers would like to thank all suppliers of props used in this
book, which have been previously credited.

Published and Distributed in the United Kingdom by
Octopus Publishing Group
Endeavour House
189 Shaftesbury Avenue
London WC2H 8JY
United Kingdom
phone (+44) (0) 207 632 5400; fax (+44) (0) 207 632 5405
info@octopus-publishing.co.uk;
www.octopusbooks.co.uk

Printed and bound in China

International foreign language rights, Brian Cearnes,
ACP Books bcearnes@acpmagazines.com.au

A catalogue record for this book is available from
the British Library.

ISBN 978-1-903777-77-0

© ACP Magazines Ltd 2010